AF538805

V&A Pattern
Digital Pioneers

V&A Publishing

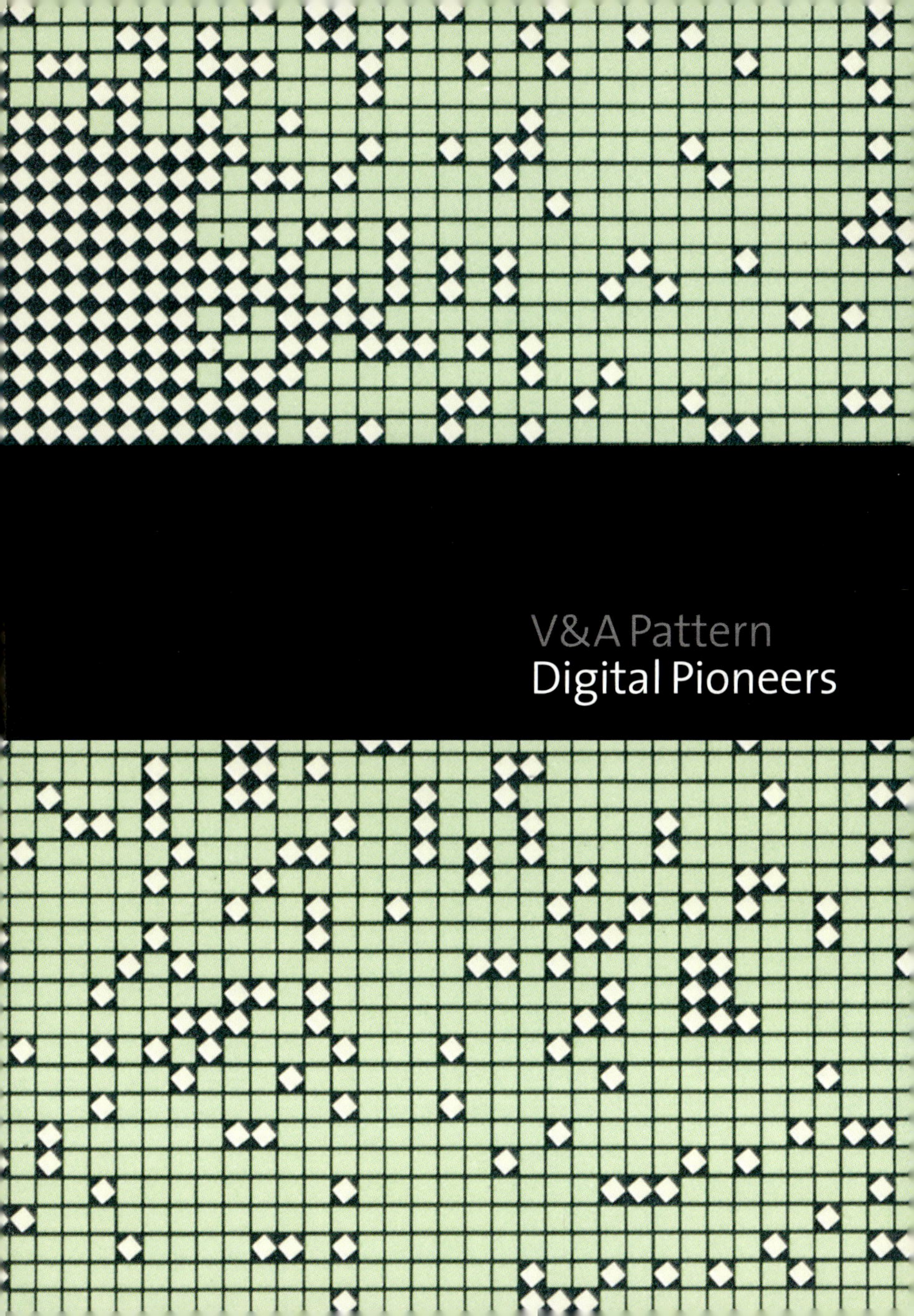
V&A Pattern
Digital Pioneers

First published by V&A Publishing, 2009
V&A Publishing
Victoria and Albert Museum
South Kensington
London SW7 2RL

First Published in India, 2009
by Roli Books Pvt. Ltd.
M-75 Greater Kailash-II (Market),
New Delhi 110 048, India.
Phone: ++91-11-4068 2000
Fax: ++91-11-2921 7185
Email: info@rolibooks.com
Website: www.rolibooks.com

The moral right of the author(s) has been asserted.

ISBN 978-81-7436-717-4
Library of Congress Control Number 2009923090

10 9 8 7 6 5 4 3 2 1
2013 2012 2011 2010 2009

A catalogue record for this book is available
from the British Library.

Design: Rose
New V&A Photography by Lauren Mclean,
V&A Photographic Studio

Front cover (A):
Mark Wilson, *e4708* (detail), plate 45.
Pages 2–3 (B):
Aaron Marcus, *Urbane Nova* (detail), plate 25.
Page 6 (C):
Paul Brown, *Swimming Pool* (detail).
Giclée print (artist's proof), 57.2 x 82.2 cm.
UK, 1997 (V&A: E.994–2008)
Page 11 (D):
Herbert W. Franke, *Untitled* (detail) from the
series DRAKULA. Lithograph, 28.2 x 20.3 cm.
Austria, 1971 (V&A: E.182–2008)
Pages 78–9 (E):
Mark Wilson, *e4708* (detail), plate 45.

Letters in (brackets) refer to the file name of the
images on the accompanying disc.

Printed in China

V&A Publishing
Victoria and Albert Museum
South Kensington
London SW7 2RL
www.vam.ac.uk

In 2007 the V&A and Birkbeck College, University of London were jointly awarded a grant from the Arts and Humanities Research Council (AHRC) to research the development of computer-based art. Further information regarding this research can be found on the project website: www.technocultures.org.uk

We gratefully acknowledge the support of the AHRC

We are also grateful to several other groups and individuals who have kindly supported this ongoing project, as well as several generous donors to the Victoria and Albert Museum:

Given by the American Friends of the V&A through the generosity of Patric Prince: plates 1, 2, 3, 6, 7, 8, 10, 15, 16, 17, 18, 21, 22, 27, 28, 30, 33, 34, 35, 36 and page 6 (detail)

Given by the Computer Arts Society, supported by System Simulation Ltd, London: plates 4, 5, 9, 13, 14, 19, 20, 23, 24, 29 and page 11 (detail)

Given by the artist: plates 25, 26, 31, 40, 41, 42, 43, 44 and 45

V&A Pattern

Each *V&A Pattern* book is an introduction to the Victoria and Albert Museum's extraordinarily diverse design archives. The museum has more than three million designs for textiles, decorations, wallpapers and prints; some well-known, others less so. This series explores pattern-making in all its forms, across the world and through the centuries. The books are intended to be both beautiful and useful – showing patterns to enjoy in their own right and as inspiration for new design.

V&A Pattern presents the greatest names and styles in design, while also highlighting the work of anonymous draughtsmen and designers, often working unacknowledged in workshops, studios and factories, and responsible for designs of aesthetic originality and technical virtuosity. Many of the most interesting and imaginative designs are seen too rarely. *V&A Pattern* gathers hidden treasures – from pattern books, swatch books, company archives, design records and catalogues – to form a fascinating introduction to the variety and beauty of pattern at the V&A.

The compact disc at the back of each book invites you to appreciate the ingenuity of the designs, and the endless possibilities for their application. To use the images professionally, you need permission from V&A Images, as the V&A controls – on behalf of others – the rights held in its books and CD-Roms. *V&A Pattern* can only ever be a tiny selection of the designs available at www.vandaimages.com. We see requests to use images as an opportunity to help us to develop and improve our licensing programme – and for us to let you know about images you may not have found elsewhere.

Digital Pioneers
Honor Beddard and Douglas Dodds

In the years that followed World War Two, access to computers ceased to be restricted solely to the military. As they became more accessible in laboratories and universities, a small group of scientists and programmers were joined by artists and designers who began to realize the creative potential of the new technology. Computers offered the opportunity to explore innovative ways of creating images that would demonstrate a hitherto unexpected purity in their natural patterning, symmetry and order.

The earliest work in this selection, *Oscillon 40* (1952, plate 1), was actually produced on an analogue cathode-ray oscilloscope. The artist, Ben Laposky, manipulated the electronic wave forms displayed on the screen and then photographed the results. Laposky created some of the first graphics generated using an electronic machine and helped to pave the way for the truly digital pioneers who followed. Herbert Franke also used analogue equipment to produce some of his early works, but went on to exploit the capabilities of the emerging digital computer technology.

Many of the earliest computer-generated images were created by people who trained initially in science or mathematics, such as Herbert W. Franke, Frieder Nake and Georg Nees. These first practitioners were faced with cumbersome computers that often lacked a screen or user interface. Instead, they relied upon carefully constructed programs, or algorithms, which they used as instructions to drive a simple printer or plotter, a machine with a mechanical arm that guides a pen across the drawing surface. The limitations of these devices contribute to the minimal, geometric aesthetic of many of the early works, but their apparent simplicity often belies the complexity of their creation. Frieder Nake's *Hommage à Paul Klee, 13/9/65 Nr. 2* (plate 6), for example, was one of the most elaborate pieces of algorithmic art of its day.

As artists became familiar with the new technologies, they began to experiment with writing random variables into their programs, introducing genuine autonomy into the creative process. In *Random War* (plate 11), Charles Csuri deliberately uses a random number generator to distribute and position the computer-generated images of toy soldiers. The lithograph illustrated here derives from a much larger work that includes the names of soldiers who – according to the program – were killed, wounded, missing, awarded a medal or survived.

For some artists, an analytical approach to their work predates the arrival of the new technology. For example, Manfred Mohr's early paintings share a systematic aesthetic with his later plotter drawings. Computers enabled him to work with a level of computational complexity that was impossible for humans to achieve unaided. For the past 30 years, Mohr's art has explored the logical deconstruction of the cube. Similarly, Vera Molnar works with repeating units of line and form, systematically charting their descent from order into chaos. The relationship between individual works and a much larger series of variations and permutations is important, because it was only as a set that the full results of the programs could be realised. From the mid 1970s onwards, Paul Brown's generative art has used tiling and simple systems (or 'cellular automata') that are capable of evolving and propagating.

While some artists concentrated on algorithmic works, others saw the potential of computers for three-dimensional design. William Fetter's drawings of human figures were produced for the Boeing Company and established his reputation as a pioneer of computer graphics, while Robert Mallary created some of the first computer-generated sculptural works.

Artists such as Harold Cohen and Roman Verostko developed their own software and machines. Cohen was an established painter when he began to experiment with computers in the late 1960s. From the 1970s onwards, he concentrated on developing AARON, a computer program designed to generate works of art. AARON initially created black-and-white line drawings that were sometimes then hand-coloured, but the later works illustrated here were produced in full colour by the software itself. In effect, Cohen examines whether successful imagery is underpinned by a system that can be codified.

The distinctive aesthetic of Roman Verostko's plotter drawings is in part due to the development of a bespoke multi-pen plotter, driven by his own computer program. *Manchester Illuminated Universal Turing Machine, #1* (plate 39) allows us to see the very building blocks of its construction, with binary code on one side and the plotter drawing on the other. A former monk, Verostko also incorporates gold leaf in the finished work, highlighting the link with manuscript illumination.

The breadth and variety of the works included here demonstrate each artist's unique relationship with the computer. The digital pioneers' vision opened up a new field to subsequent generations of artists and designers, and continues to inspire us more than half a century later.

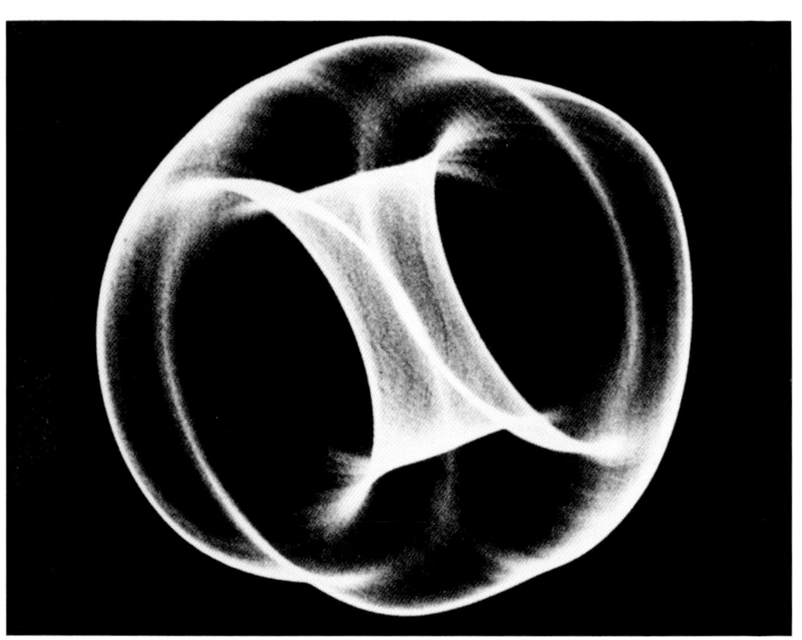

1
Ben Laposky, *Oscillon 40*
C-type print, 20.3 x 25.1 cm. USA, 1952 (V&A: E.958–2008)

2
Ben Laposky, *Oscillon 520*
C-type print, 25.5 x 20.4 cm. USA, 1960 (V&A: E.1096–2008)

3
Herbert W. Franke, *Elektronische Grafik*
Screenprint (artist's proof), 70 x 49.9 cm. Austria, 1970 (original photograph 1954/5) (V&A: E.1072–2008)

4
Herbert W. Franke, *Elektronische Grafik*
Screenprint, 68.1 x 45.8 cm. Austria, 1970 (original photograph 1954/5) (V&A: E.122–2008)

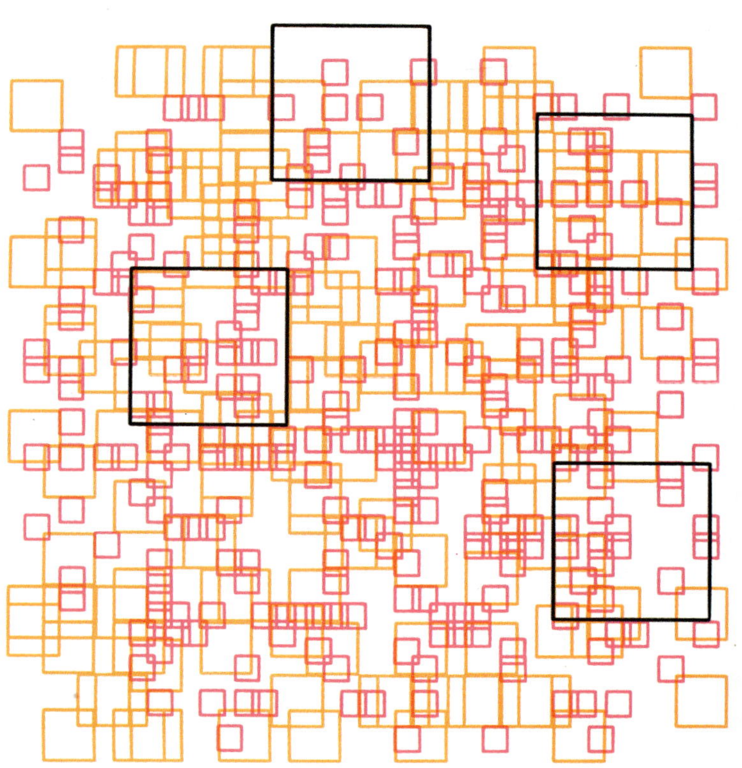

5
Herbert W. Franke, *Quadrate (Squares)*
Screenprint, 69.8 x 49.6 cm. Austria, 1969/70 (V&A: E.113–2008)

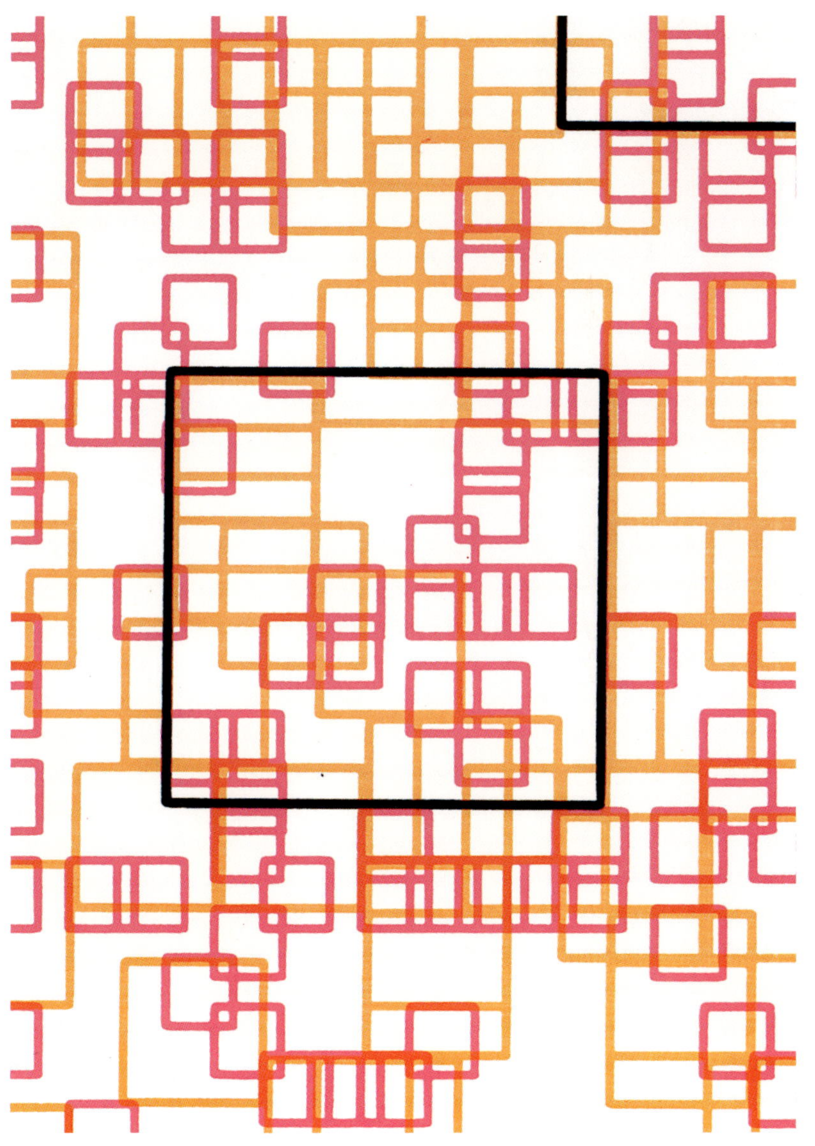

5
(detail)

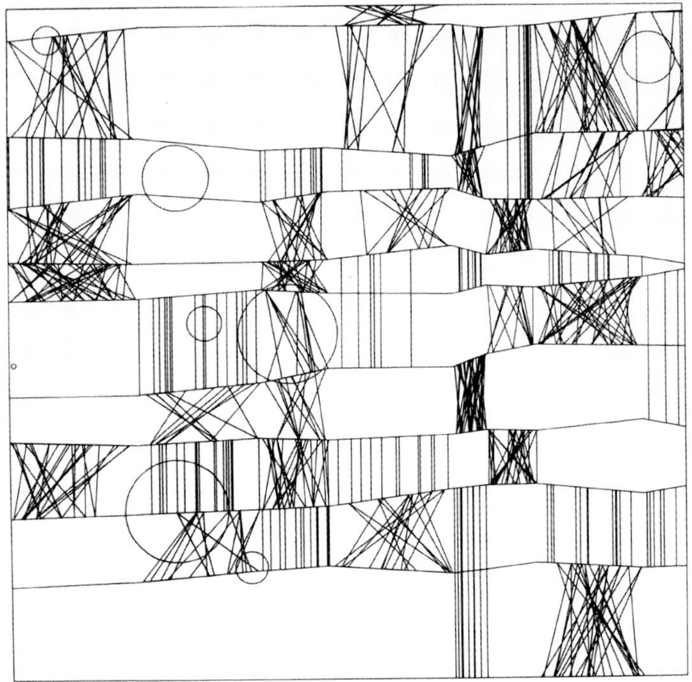

6
Frieder Nake, *Hommage à Paul Klee, 13/9/65 Nr. 2*
Screenprint (edition of 40, unnumbered), 49.2 x 49.2 cm. Germany, 1965 (V&A: E.951–2008)

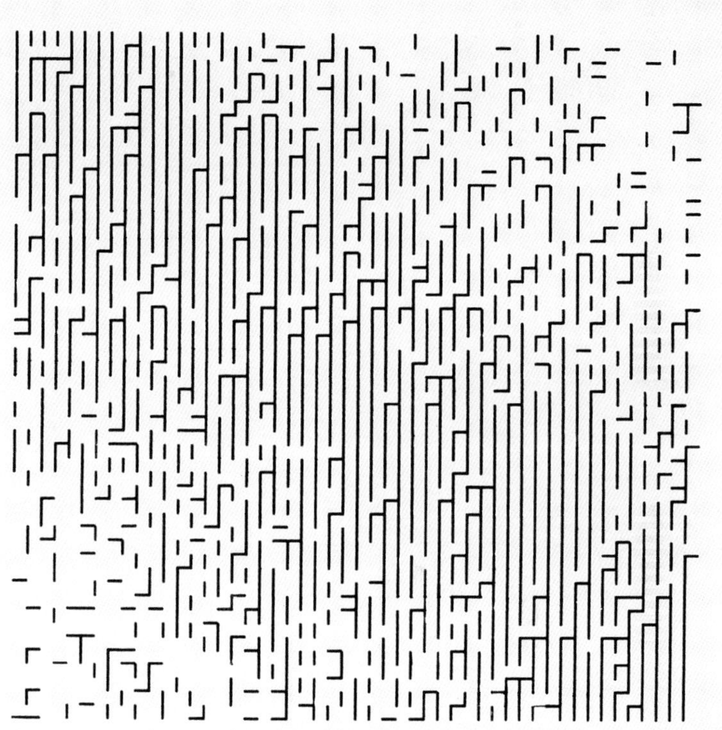

7
Frieder Nake, *Walk-through-Raster, series 2.1–4*
C-type print, 44.5 x 44.3 cm. Germany, 1966 (V&A: E.955–2008)

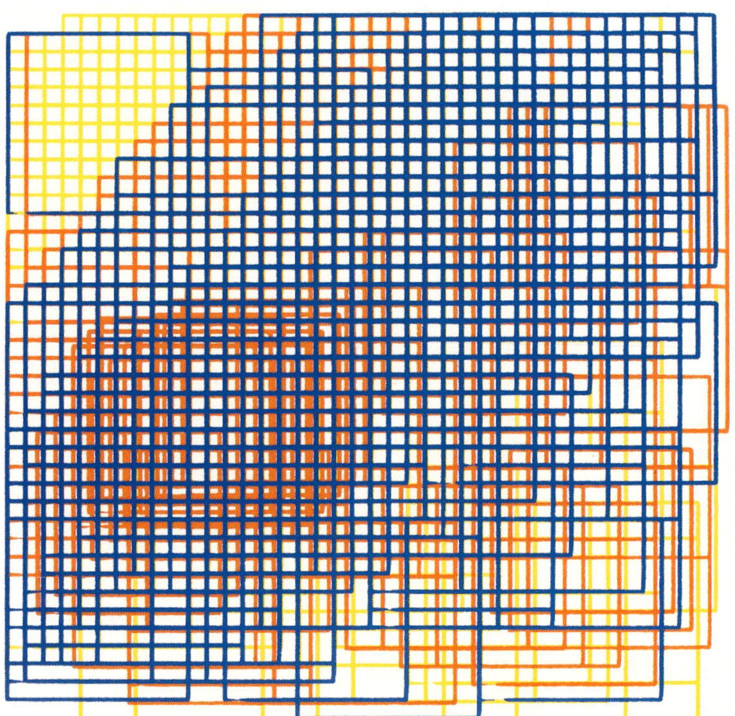

8
Frieder Nake, *Walk-through-Raster Vancouver Version*
Screenprint (edition of 25, unnumbered), 50.6 x 38.1 cm. Germany, 1972 (V&A: E.972–2008)

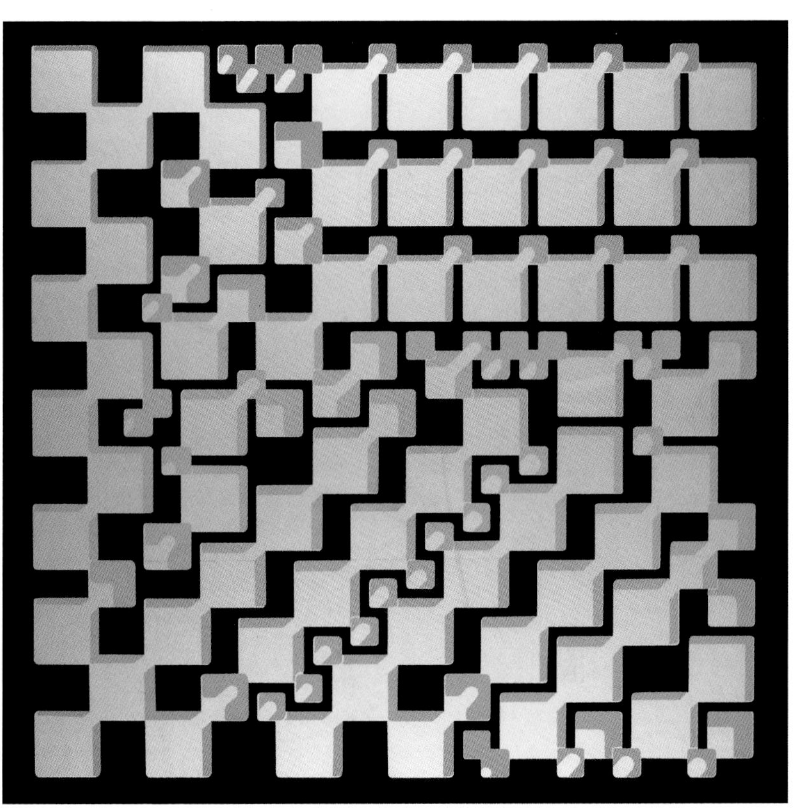

9
Georg Nees, *Plastik 1*
Screenprint, 75.4 x 68.7 cm. Germany, 1965–8 (V&A: E.61–2008)

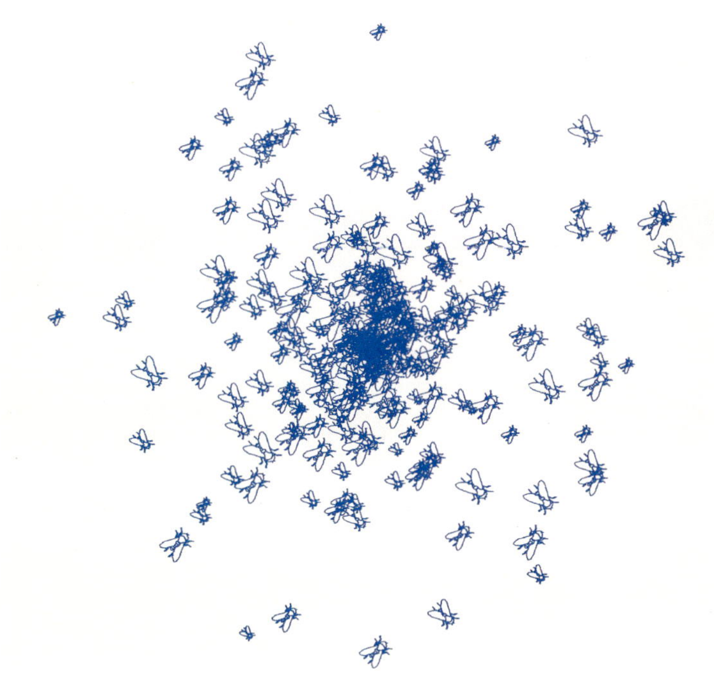

10
Charles Csuri, *Flies*
Screenprint, 35.4 x 27.8 cm. USA, 1967 (V&A: E.959–2008)

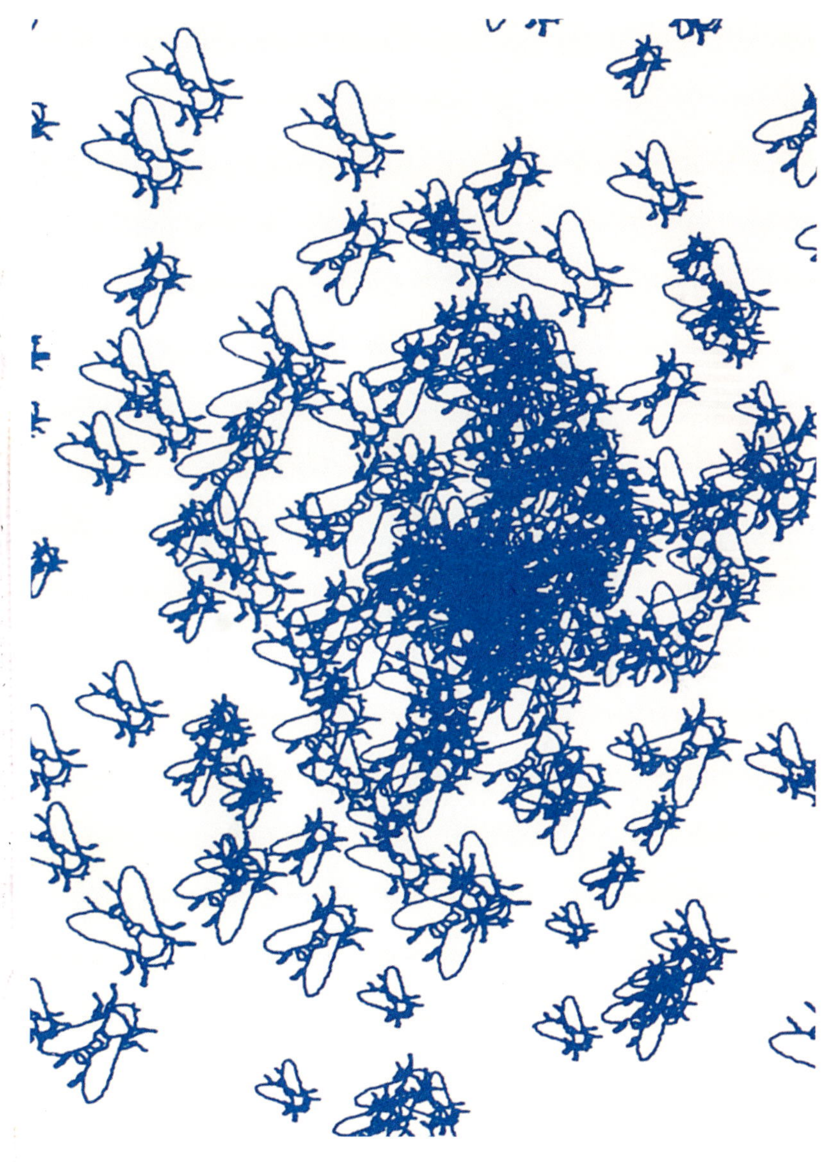

10
(detail)

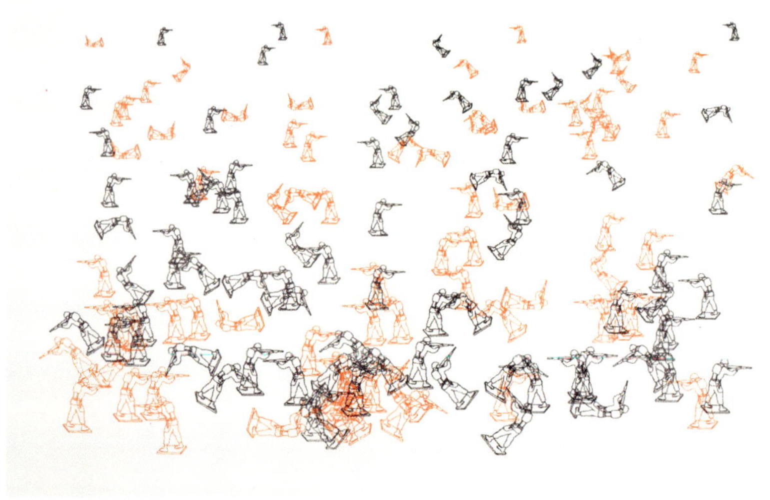

11
Charles Csuri, *Random War*
Lithograph (from the *Cybernetic Serendipity* collectors' set, Motif Editions, 1968), 50.7 x 75.4 cm. USA, 1967
(V&A: Circ.775–1969)

11
(detail)

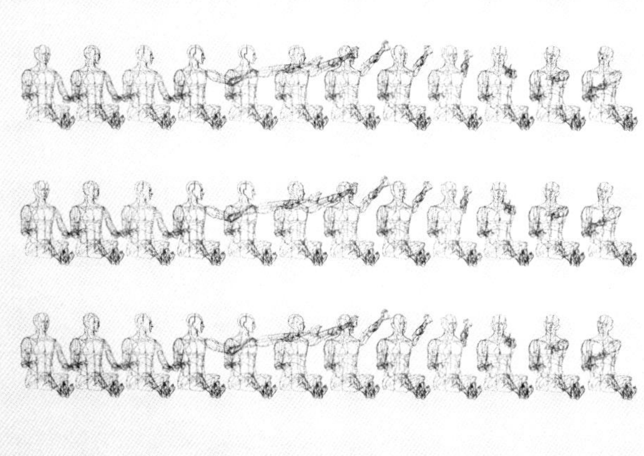

12
William Fetter, *Human Figure*
Lithograph (from the *Cybernetic Serendipity* collectors' set, Motif Editions, 1968), 50.7 x 75.4 cm. USA, 1968
(V&A: Circ.773–1969)

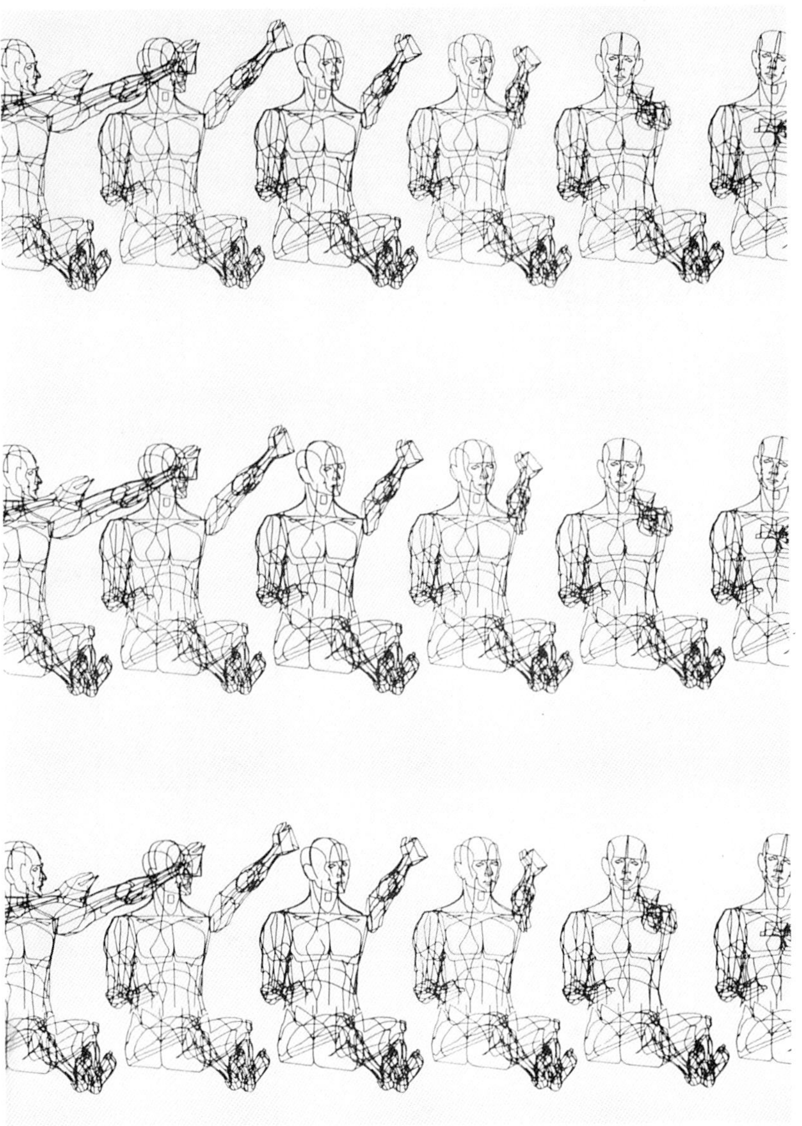

12
(detail)

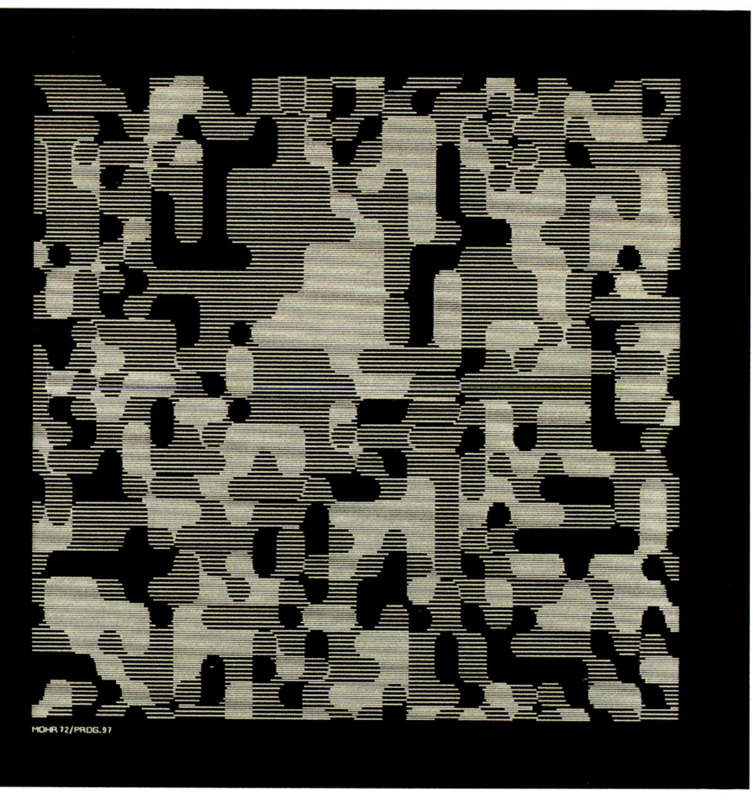

13
Manfred Mohr, *P-96 (theoretical space projection)*
Screenprint, 55.8 x 55.7 cm. Germany, 1972 (V&A: E.65–2008)

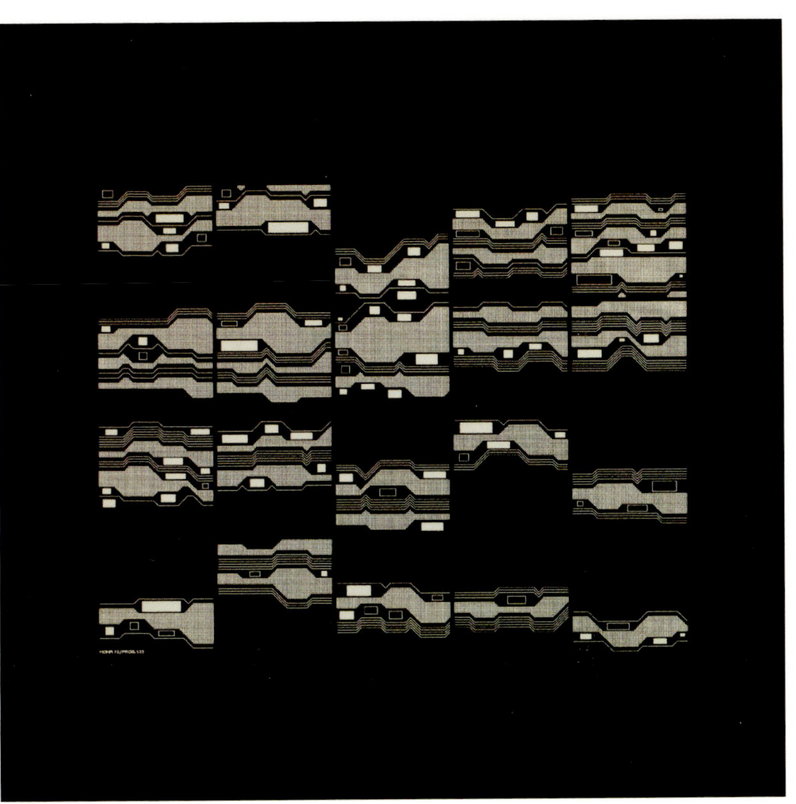

14
Manfred Mohr, *P-133 (cluster phobia)*
Screenprint, 60.1 x 59.8 cm. Germany, 1972 (V&A: E.80–2008)

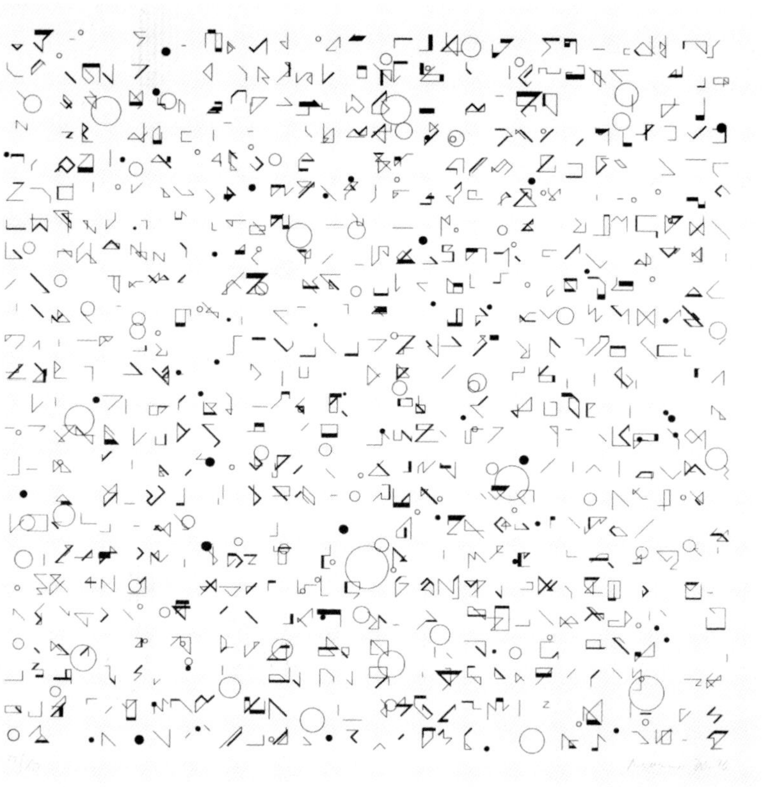

15
Manfred Mohr, *P-049*
Screenprint (51/80; *Scratch Code: 1970–1975* portfolio, Editions Média, 1976), 39.8 x 39.8 cm. Germany, 1970
(V&A: E.977:4–2008)

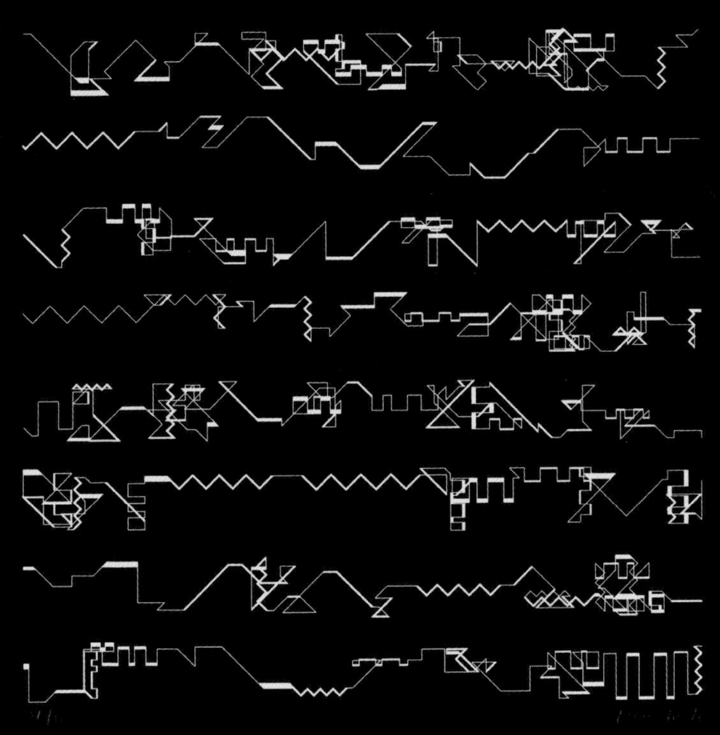

16
Manfred Mohr, *P-021*
Screenprint (51/80; *Scratch Code: 1970–1975* portfolio, Editions Média, 1976), 39.8 x 39.8 cm. Germany, 1970
(V&A: E.977:6–2008)

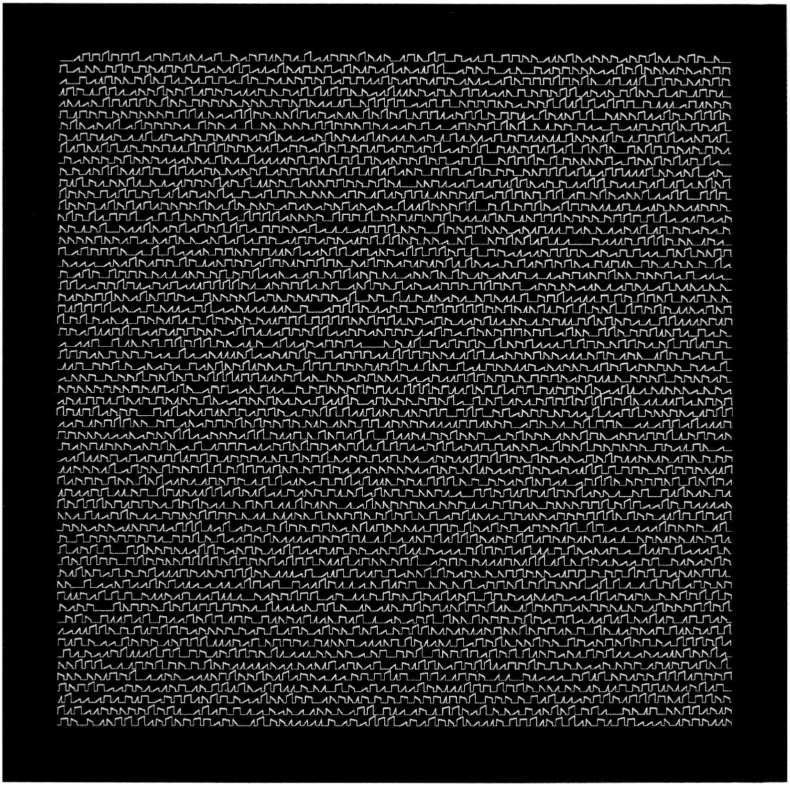

17
Manfred Mohr, *P-122*
Screenprint (51/80; *Scratch Code: 1970–1975* portfolio, Editions Média, 1976), 39.8 x 39.8 cm. Germany, 1972
(V&A: E.977:3–2008)

17
(detail)

18
Manfred Mohr, *P-155*
Screenprint (51/80; *Scratch Code: 1970–1975* portfolio, Editions Média, 1976), 39.8 x 39.8 cm. Germany, 1974
(V&A: E.977:5–2008)

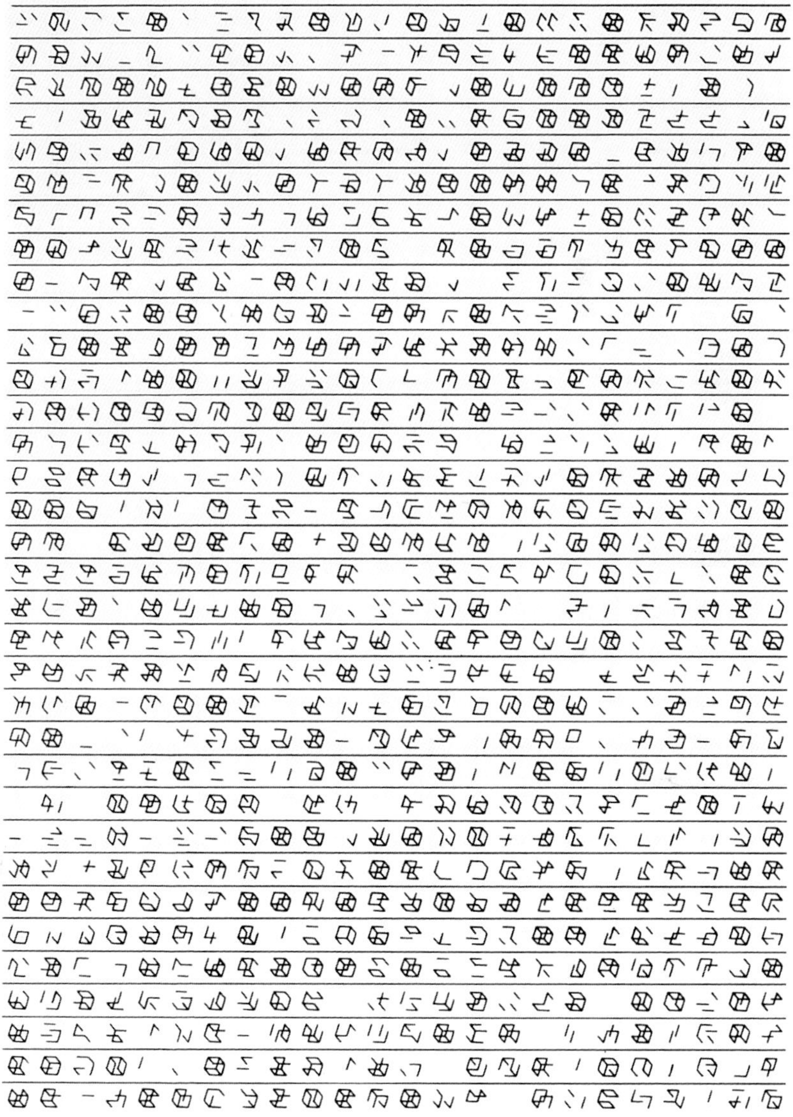

18
(detail)

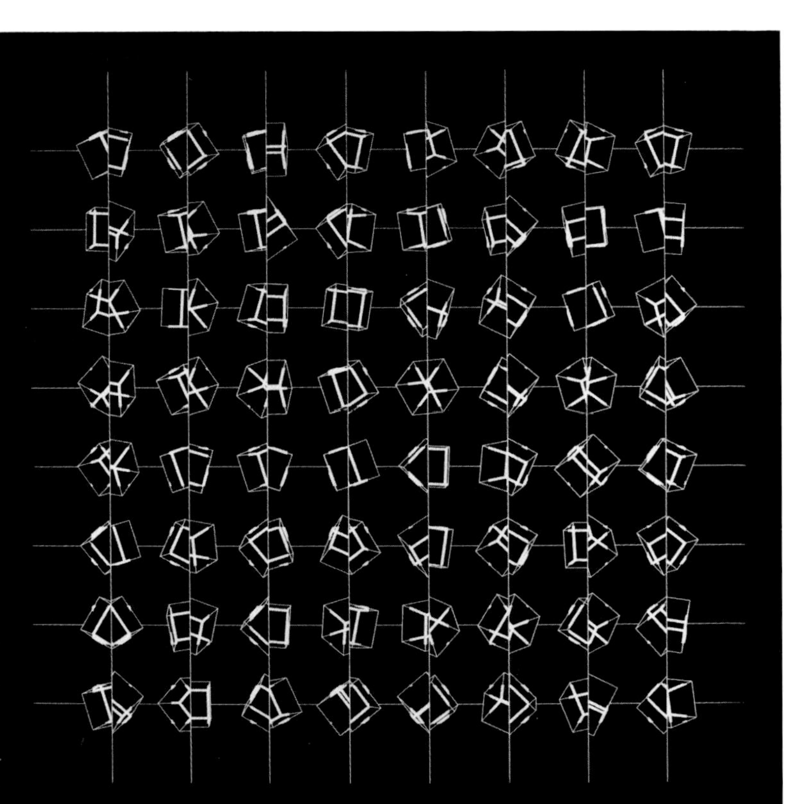

19
Manfred Mohr, *P-197*
Screenprint (artist's proof), 47.7 x 47.8 cm. Germany, 1977–9 (V&A: E.58–2008)

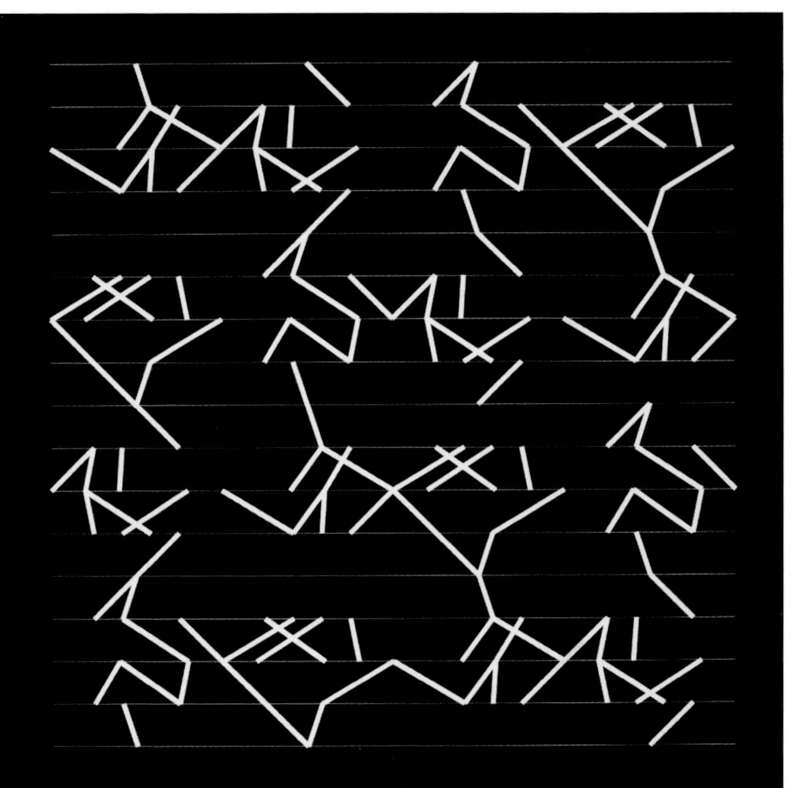

20
Manfred Mohr, *P-226a*
Photogravure (artist's proof), 60.8 x 60.6 cm. Germany, 1978 (V&A: E.207–2008)

21

Edward Zajec, *T.V.C. 20 68179 71*

Impact print, 27.9 x 28.5 cm. USA, 1971 (V&A: E.970–2008)

22
Edward Zajec, *T.V.C. 80 38839 71*
Impact print, 27.8 x 28.3 cm. USA, 1971 (V&A: E.971–2008)

23
Manuel Barbadillo, *Untitled*
Impact print, 36.7 x 34.7 cm. Spain, *c.*1972 (V&A: E.158–2008)

24
Manuel Barbadillo, *Adfera*
Screenprint (46/50), 61 x 44.8 cm. Spain, 1972 (V&A: E.194–2008)

25
Aaron Marcus, *Urbane Nova*
Lithograph (19/50), 27.8 x 21.5 cm. USA, 1972/4 (V&A: E.658–1976)

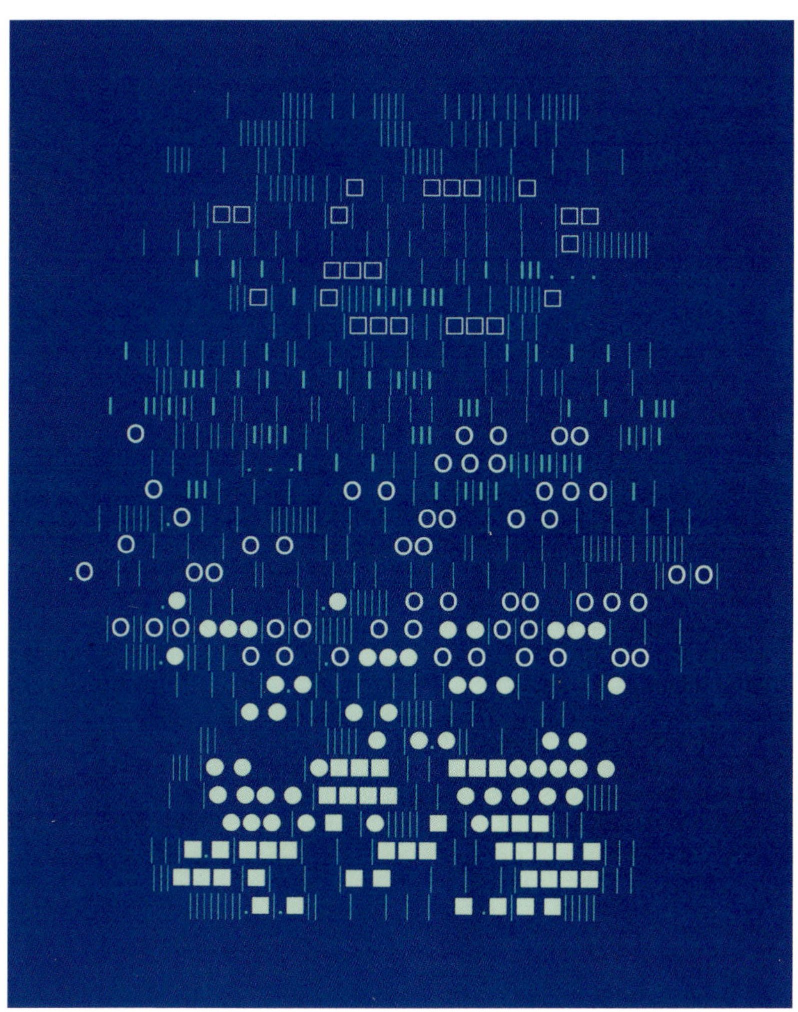

26
Aaron Marcus, *Evolving Gravity*
Lithograph (19/50), 27.8 x 21.5 cm. USA, 1972/4 (V&A: E.656–1976)

27
Paul Brown, *Untitled, Computer Assisted Drawing*
Plotter drawing, 27.6 x 26.8 cm. UK/Australia, 1975 (V&A: E.961–2008)

27
(detail)

28
Paul Brown, *A-B Modulars*
Plotter drawing, 45.7 x 42.3 cm. UK/Australia, 1977 (V&A: E.1080–2008)

28
(detail)

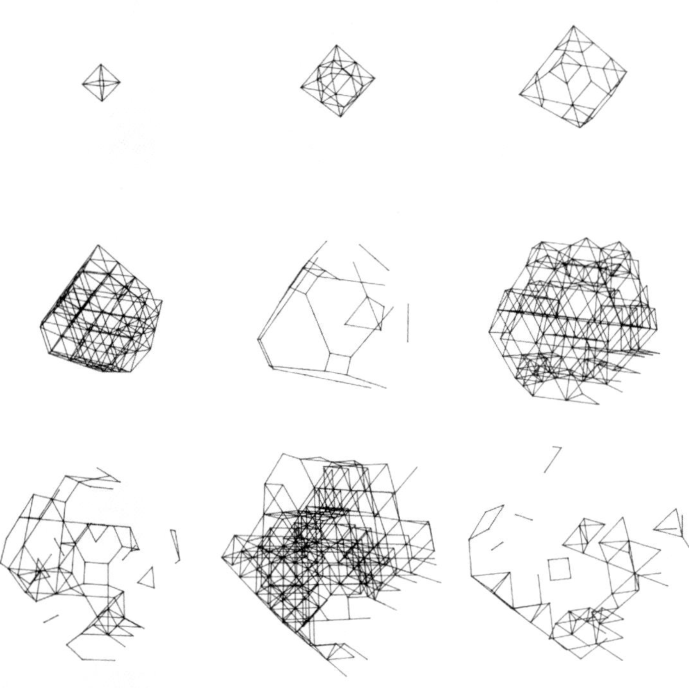

29
Paul Brown, *BIGDIM / 0 10 10 0 0 0 0 / 200, 120 / 11,969*
Plotter drawing, 51.9 x 47.7 cm. UK/Australia, 1979 (V&A: E.131–2008)

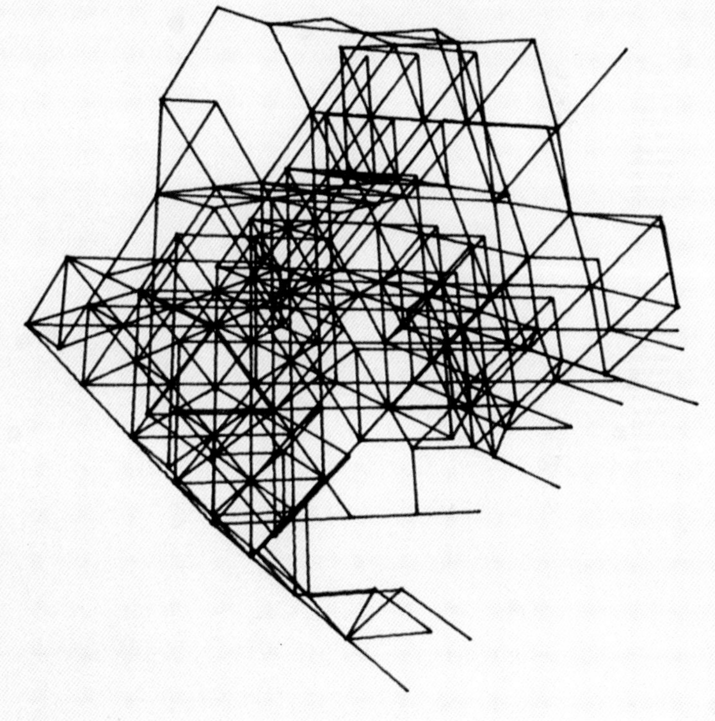

29
(detail)

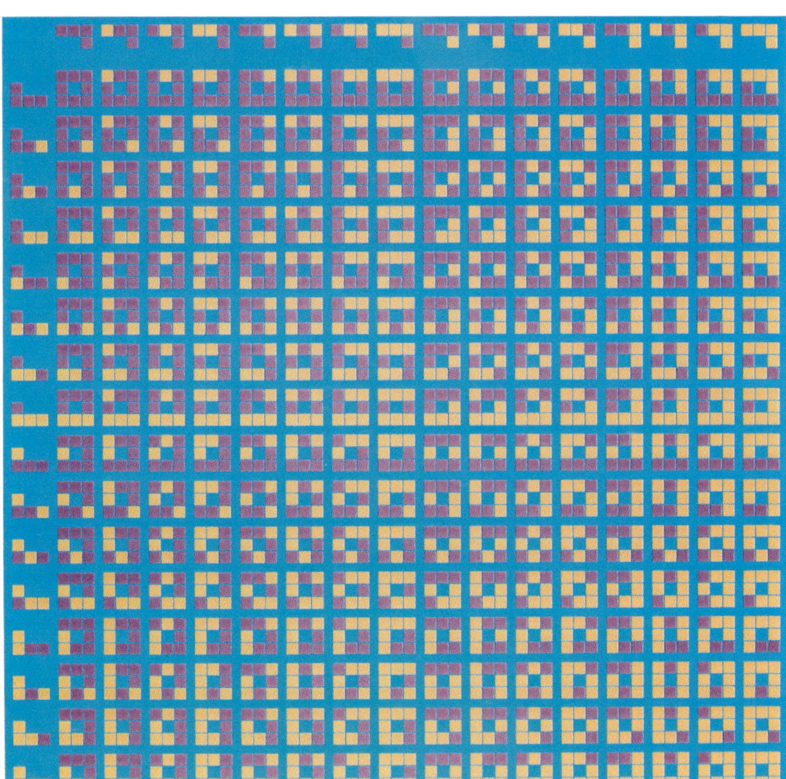

30
Paul Brown, *Neighbourhood Count*
Laser print (4/10), 41.8 x 29.6 cm. UK/Australia, 1991 (V&A: E.1066–2008)

30
(detail)

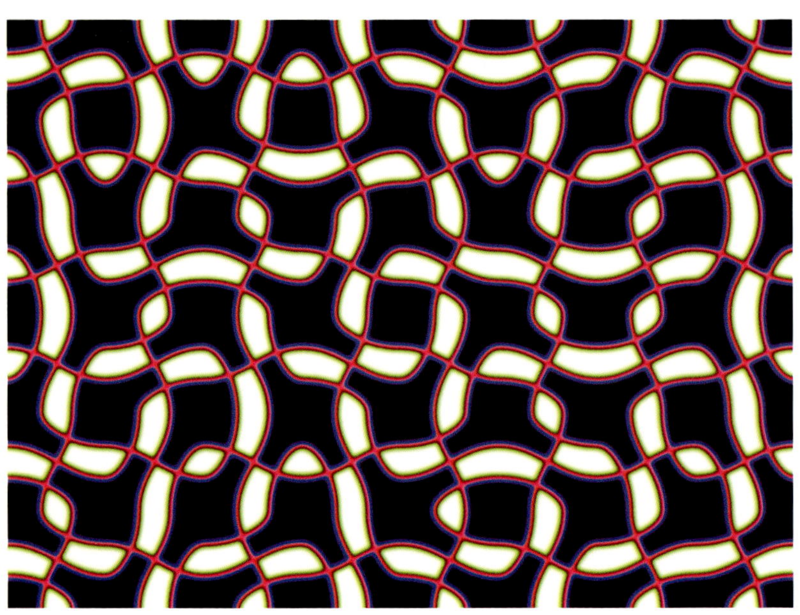

31
Paul Brown, *Gymnasts*
Giclée print (artist's proof), 60 x 80 cm. UK/Australia, 1997 (V&A: E.942–2008)

31
(detail)

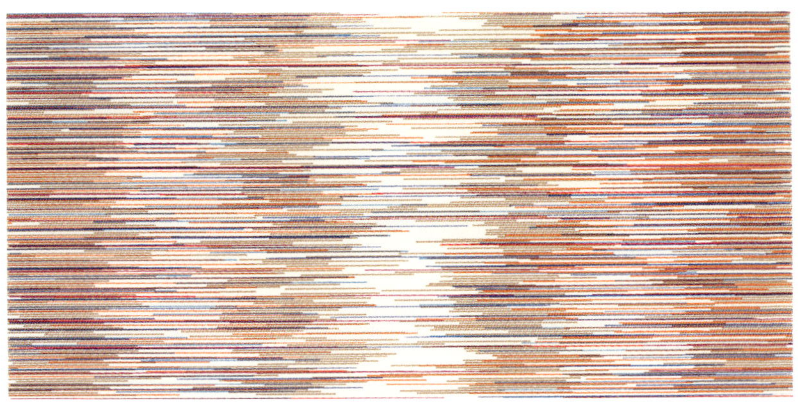

32
Vera Molnar, *Microcosmos, I. II. III. IV. V.*
Screenprint (53/100; from the portfolio *Hommage à Bartók*, Budapest/Paris 1978–9), 32.8 x 50.5 cm.
Hungary/France, 1978 (V&A: E.528–1981)

32
(detail)

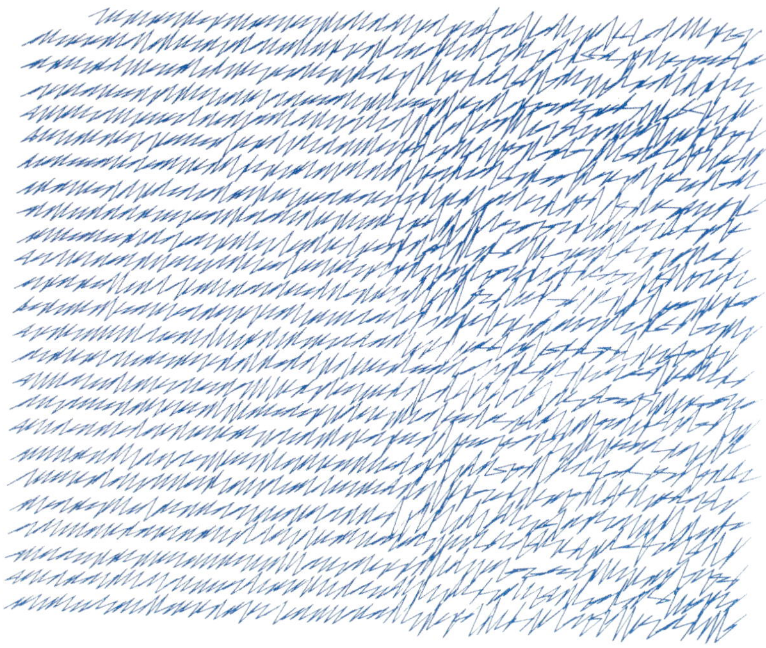

33
Vera Molnar, *Letters from my Mother*
Screenprint (artist's proof), 23.8 x 63.8 cm. Hungary/France, 1988 (V&A: E.1079–2008)

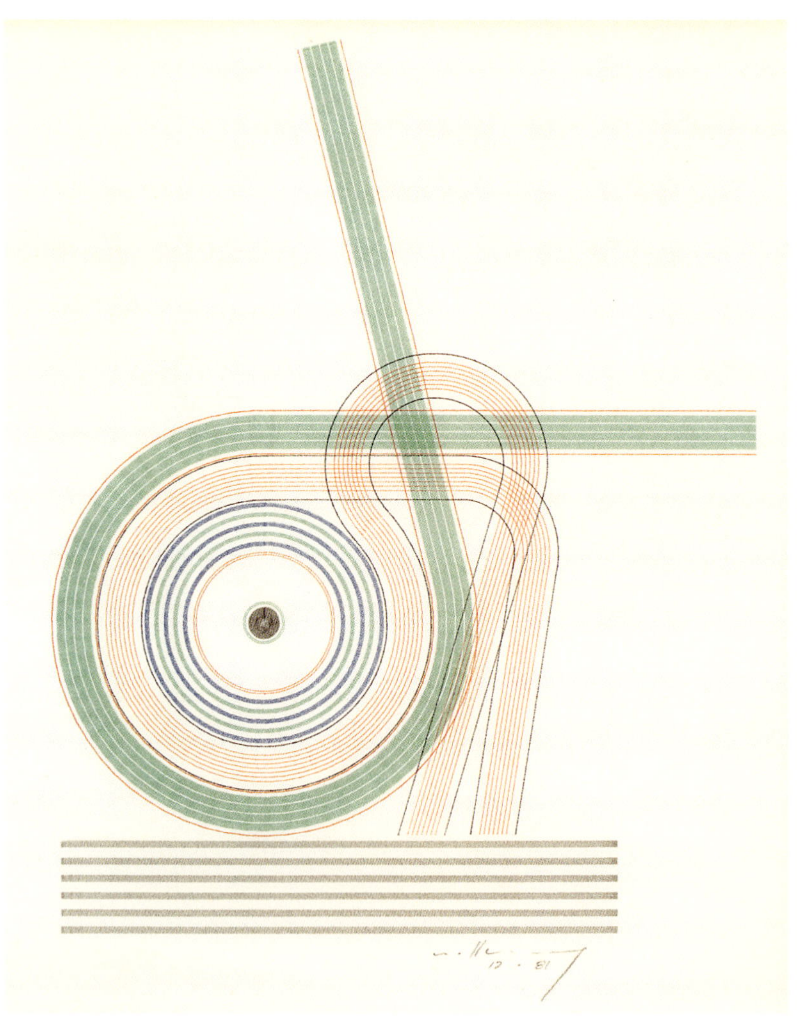

34
Robert Mallary, *Untitled*
Plotter drawing, 39.2 x 28.3 cm. USA, 1981 (V&A: E.1005–2008)

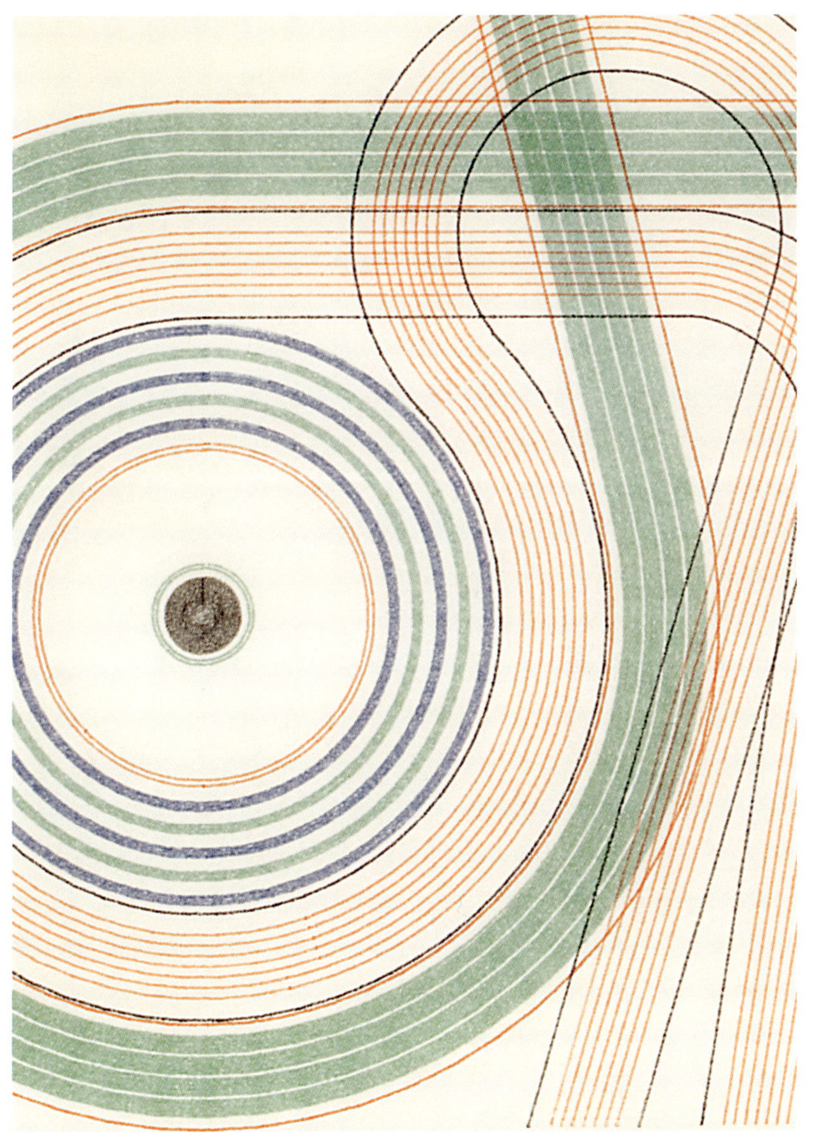

34
(detail)

The New Colossus (by E. Lazarus)
Not like the brazen giant of Greek
fame, / with conquering limbs a-
stride from land to land; / Here at
our seawashed sunset gates shall
stand / A mighty woman with a torch
whose flame / is the imprisoned
lightning, and her name / Mother
of Exiles. From her beacon-hand /
Glows world-wide welcome; her
mild eyes command / The airbridged
harbor that twin cities frame. /
"Keep ancient lands, your storied
pomp!" cries she / with silent lips.
"Give me your tired, your poor, /
Your huddled masses yearning to
breathe free, / The wretched re-
fuse of your teeming shore. / Send
these, the homeless, tempest-
tost to me, / I lift my lamp beside
the golden door!" (This poem was
written in 1883 by American poet
Emma Lazarus, and in 1903 it was in-
scribed on a bronze plaque in the
pedestal of the statue of Liberty,
a gift of the French people to the
United States, designed by Fred-
eric Auguste Bartholdi using an
iron framework by Gustave Eiffel,
dedicated in 1886 by US President
Grover Cleveland on Liberty (then
Bedloe's) Island, New York Harbor.
An extensive restoration of this
statue has been coordinated with
its 1986 Centennial celebration)
©1986 Ken Knowlton Sunnyvale CA

35
Ken Knowlton, *Statue of Liberty and Lazarus' Poem*
Digital print, 50.5 x 40.5 cm. USA, 1986 (V&A: E.948–2008)

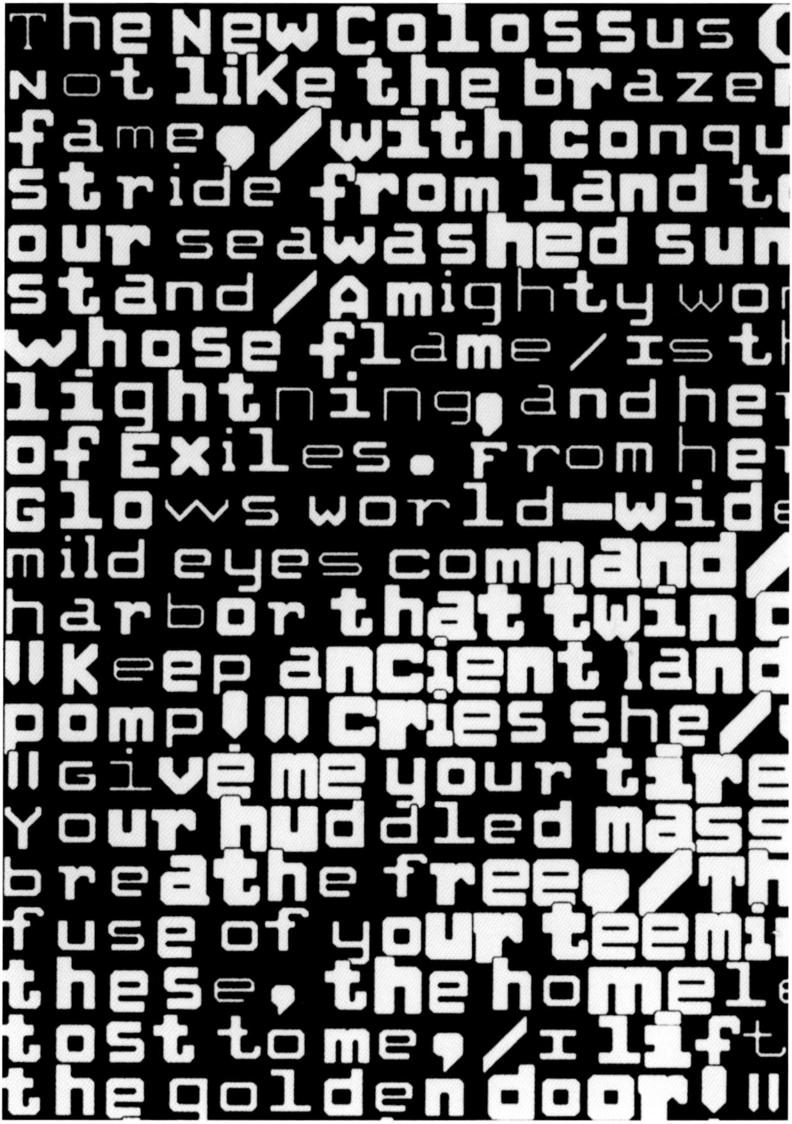

The New Colossus (
Not like the braze
fame, / with conqu
stride from land t
our seawashed sun
stand / A mighty wo
whose flame / Is th
lightning, and he
of Exiles. From he
Glows world-wide
mild eyes command /
harbor that twin
"Keep ancient land
pomp!" cries she /
"Give me your tire
Your huddled mass
breathe free, / Th
fuse of your teemi
these, the homel
tost to me, / I lift
the golden door!"

35
(detail)

36
Roman Verostko, *Pathway Series*
Multi-pen plotter drawing, 57.3 x 61.2 cm. USA, 1987 (V&A: E.956–2008)

36
(detail)

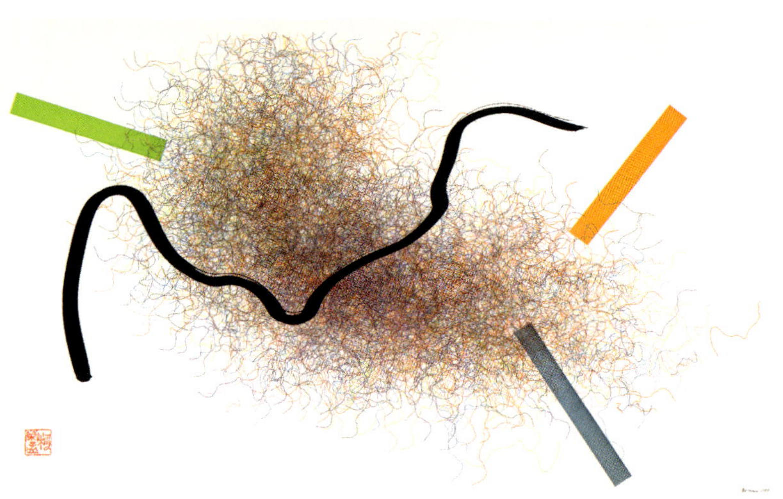

37
Roman Verostko, *Pathway Series, Bird 2*
Multi-pen plotter drawing with oriental brush, 60.9 x 100.3 cm. USA, 1990 (V&A: E.943–2008)

38
Roman Verostko, *Cyberflower, Sunshine I*
Multi-pen plotter drawing, 73.7 x 58.4 cm. USA, 2008 (V&A: E.945–2008)

39
Roman Verostko, *Manchester Illuminated Universal Turing Machine, #1*
Multi-pen plotter drawing with gold leaf, 55.9 x 76.2 cm. USA, 1998 (V&A: E.944–2008)

u=1000000000101110100110100010010101011010001101000101000001101 0
1001101000101010010111010000110100010100101011010010011101001010010010111101010
0011101010100100101011101010100110100010100010101101000001101001000001010110 1
0001001110100101000010101110100100011101001010100001011101001010011010000100 0
0111010100001110101000010010011101000101010110101001010110100000110101010100101
1010010010001101000000001101000000111010100101010101110100001001110100101010 1
0101010111010000101010111010000101000101110100010100110100100001010011010010 1
0010011010010001011101010001011101001001010111010010100011101010010100100111 01
0101010000110100101010101110101001000101101010000101101010001001101010101010 0
0101101001010100100101011010010010111010101001010111101010010100111010101000011
1010001001001010111010101001010111010101000001110101001000001101010101001011 1
0101001010110100010010001110100000001110100101001010101011101001010010010101 1
1010000010101110100001000111010000010101001110100001010011101000000100010111 01
0001000011101000010010100111010001000010110100010100101110100010100101101001 0
0000101101000101010010011101000101010111010010000011101001001010101011101010
1010011010010001010110100100100101101000000001011010000010001101000001001011 01
0000000001101001010001011101001010100011010010100101011010000010011101001010 1
0010110100100111010100000010101110101000000110101010001010101101001010101101 0
1000010101110101001001010111010100010010110101001000010111010000001110101001 0
0010110101001010010110101010100010111010100101010010111010101000001011101010100000 1
0111010000000111010101000010101110100101010110101000010111010100010101011 101
0101001001011101010101000011101010000000111010010010000111010010010001011010 10
1010100111010000000001011010010000110101010101001011101001000011010010001010 10
1110100001000111010001000011101000011010000000101101000000100101110101010010 10
1011101000100010010111010000001001110101010011010000010101011010000100001110100
1000010001110101010101010100111010000100100111010001001000011101000010100101 101
0000101000011101010101010101110100010010011010001001001101010010100101110100 0
1000101011101000000011101000100100101110100110100100100001011010101010011010 0
0101000101110100001101010000100010111010100110101010010100101101010100110100 10
0101011101001110100100000010110100010101010001110100100001010110100000010011010
0100010010111010010000110101000001001011101001001010011010010010101010110100110
1001001010010110100110100101000001011010010000011101010010011010101010000101 1
1010010100000101110100101010101110101000100101101001001110100101010001011101 00
0100111010100001011010010011101001010101010111010010001110100101010100101110 1
0010001110101000001010101110011010100000101101001001110101000000101110100101 1
0101000001010110100101001011101010000100101110100001101010001000010110101001 1
0101000100010110101010101001011101010001010010110100010101011101001000010101 1
0101000101110101001001010101110101010010010111010100011101000111010100100101 0
0101110101000111010100101000101110101000101110101000010010111010100011101000 1
0100010111010010100101110101001010100101110100101010101010111010100001010101 01
1010000100111010000101010101011101010100010111010101000101011101000000111 01
0101000100101110101000000111010101001000101110101000000110101000010110100000011
1010010000001011101010001110101001000101011101010011010101000101011010000001
1010101010010101011010000000100110101010100100111010100110101010100100101101 01
0011010010010011101000001101010101010010101101010001001101000101001010101110 1
0000011010101010101001011010001000111010001010101010110100010001110100001010 1
0111010001001000011101001101000000010011101000000100101110100010001010011101 0
0000010010111010010101010010110100001010101011101000100101001011101000000100
0101110101010010110100010001001110100000100101011101000000101010111010000 1000 1
1100111010000100000111010000100100111010000010100101110100000101001011010000
1000101011101000010001001101000100001110101110100001001001011101000001001001 0
1110100000001010111010000101010001101000100101110100001000001110100001001110 1
0001000000101110101010010110100010000010111010000101010101110100000010101011 10
1000100001010111010001000010101110100100001110101001001001101000000101011101
0001000100101110101010000111010100101011010010101000011010000010100110100000
0001110100000100100111010010110100100010100101101010100110100010100100101101 0
1010011010000101000010110011010100100101110101010011010001010101010110011010 1
0001010101100110100100010101011101010001000111010010010101010101101001010010 1
0001101001000000101110100000110101001010101101001010101010110100100010000101 1 1
0100010101011010100000101011010001000001101001000101011010000100111010100101 0
1010101110100101101001001000101011001101001001001010101110100110100100100101 0
1101001011010010010010010111010010110100100101000101100110100100101001010111 01
0001010111010010010111001010010010101001011100110100101000101010111010001000
1110100001010010110100101000101110100101000101101000100111010010100010010111
1010001001110100101001000101110011010010001000111010001001110100101001010101 1
1001101001010000011100110101010101011010000000111010010101001010101110100100 0
1110100101010010101110011010000101001001100110101000001101000000011101001010 1
0100101011100110101000100001101000000001110100010010101010111010001000111010 10
1010101010101101000010011101001000100101011101001010100001001101010000000010110
1001001110101000010101110100100001101010000000010110100100011101010010010111 01
0000110101000010101011010100010111010100001010010111010100010111010100010101 0
10111001101010001010110100001101010001001010

40
James Faure Walker, *Proposition V: Green*
Composite inkjet print, 70.2 x 100.2 cm. UK, 1991 (V&A: E.941–2008)

40
(detail)

41
AARON, a computer program written by Harold Cohen, *030508*
Digital print (2/3), 177.2 x 123.1 cm. UK/USA, 2003 (V&A: E.264–2005)

42
AARON, a computer program written by Harold Cohen, *030503*
Digital print (2/5), 127 x 90 cm. UK/USA, 2003 (V&A: E.263–2005)

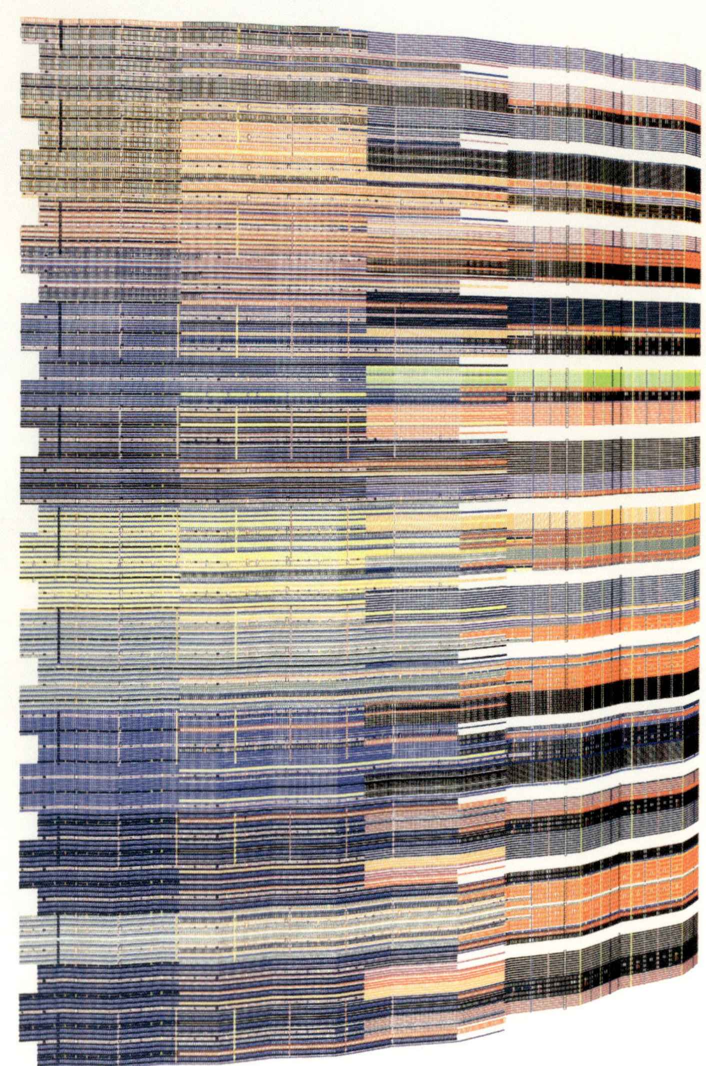

43
Mark Wilson, *PSC31*
Digital inkjet print (5/5), 111.4 x 91.8 cm. USA, 2003 (V&A: E.533–2008)

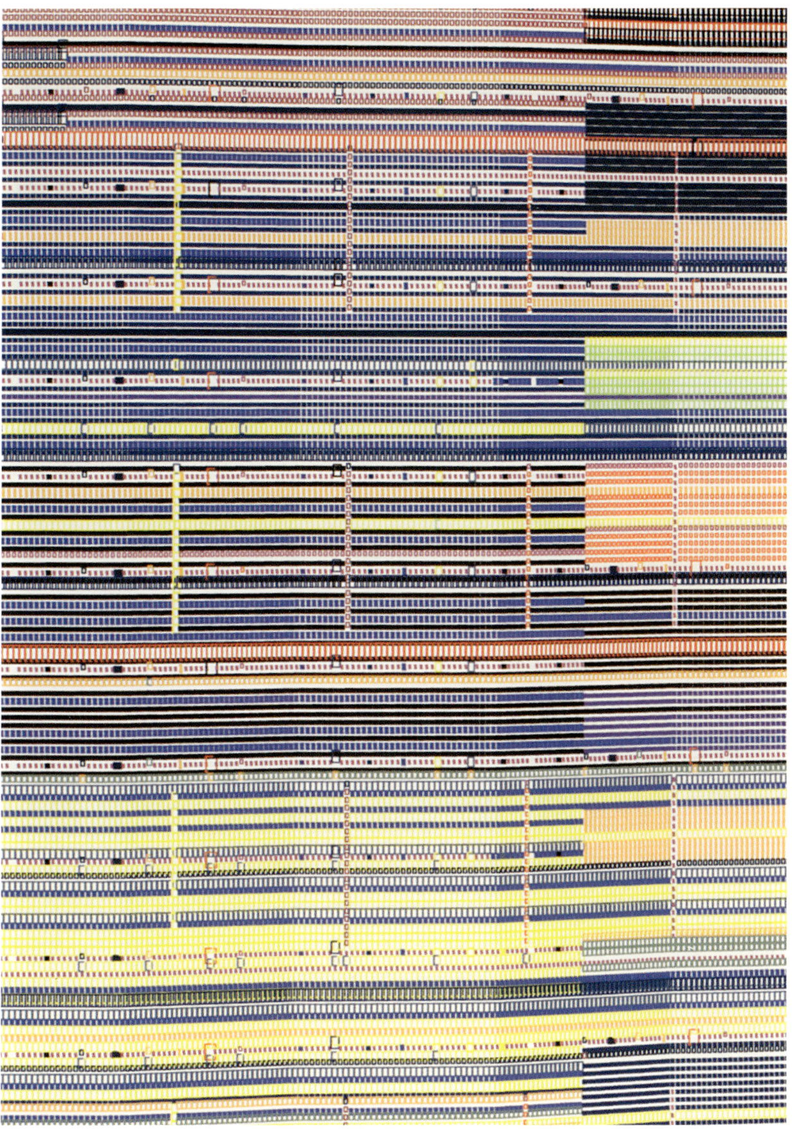

43
(detail)

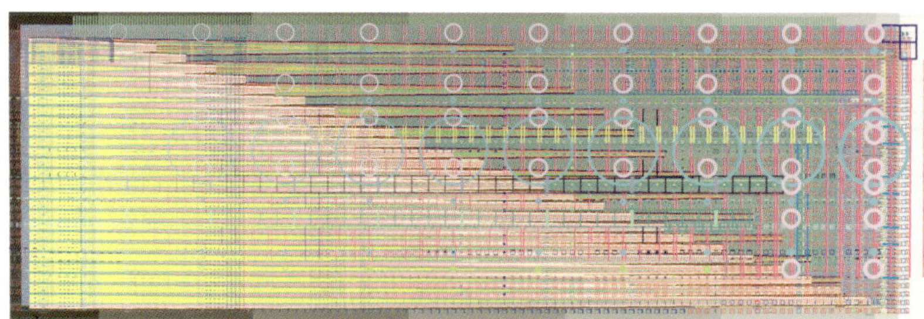

44
Mark Wilson, *p9303*
Digital inkjet print (1/5), 60.9 x 189.6 cm. USA, 2007 (V&A: E.534–2008)

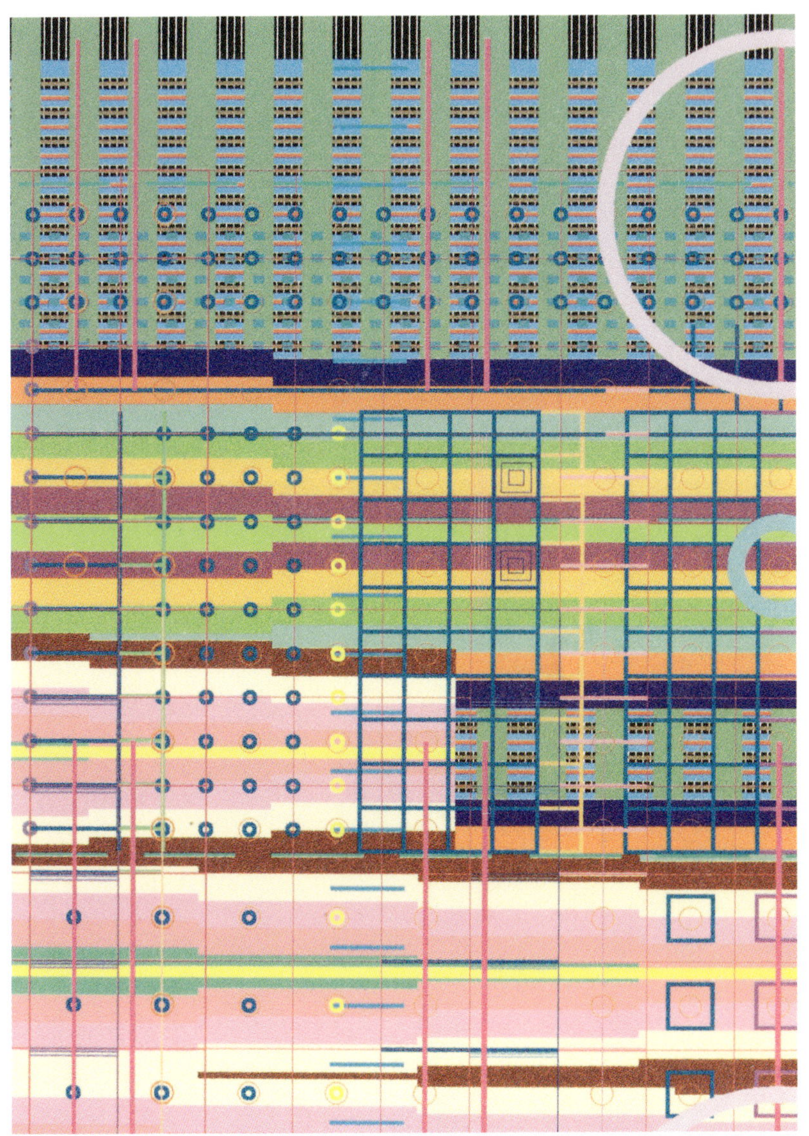

44
(detail)

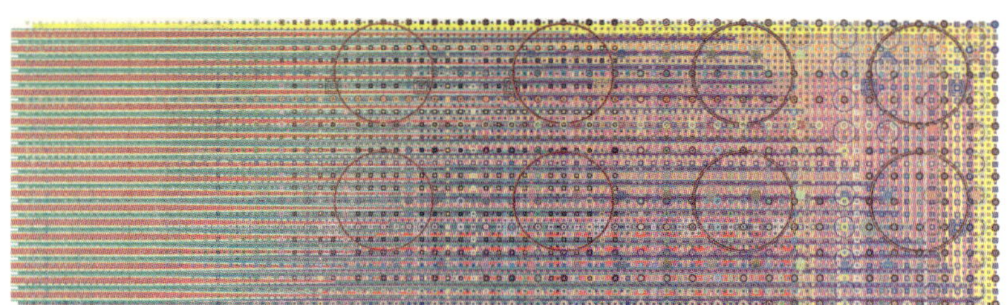

45
Mark Wilson, *e4708*
Digital inkjet print (1/5), 60.9 x 190.5 cm. USA, 2008 (V&A: E.535–2008)

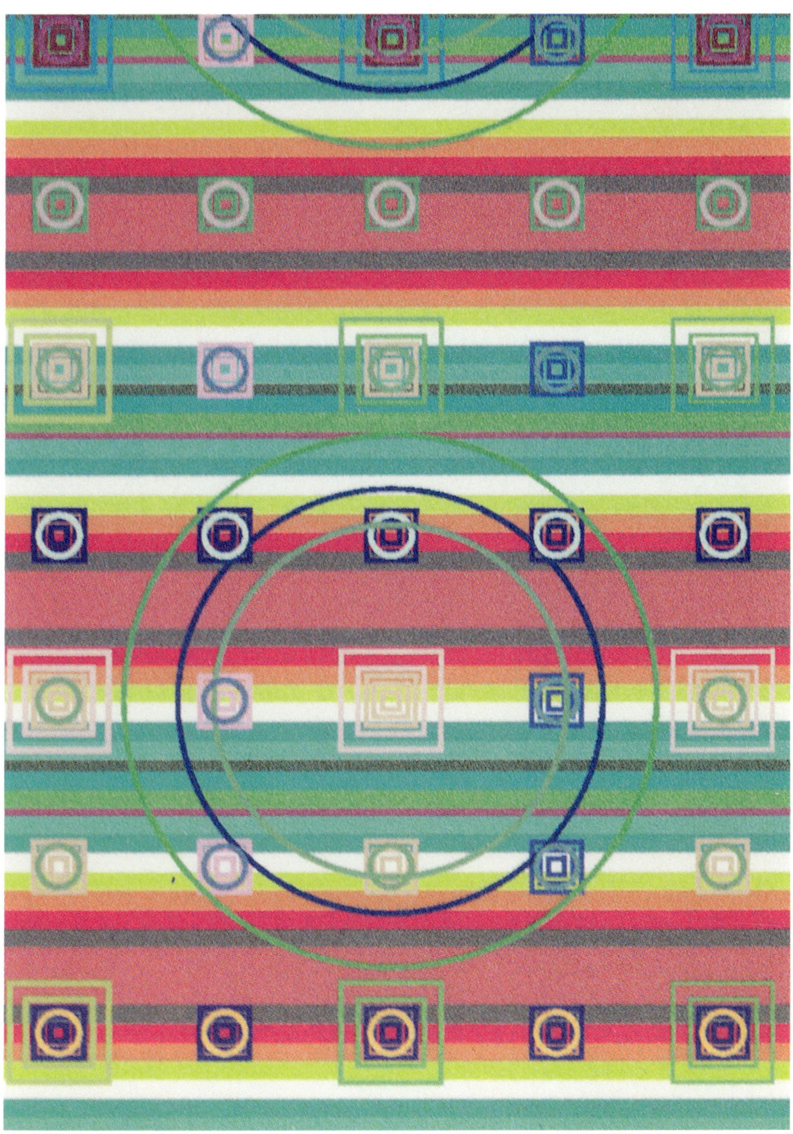

45
(detail)

Further Reading

Brown, Paul, and others, eds
White Heat, Cold Logic: British Computer Art 1960–1980
Cambridge, MA, 2009

Dietrich, Frank
Visual Intelligence: the First Decade of Computer Art (1965–1975)
In *Leonardo*, vol.19, no.2 (1986). pp.159–69

Franke, Herbert W., trans Gustav Metzger
Computer Graphics, Computer Art
London, 1971

Gere, Charlie
Digital Culture
London, 2002

Herzogenrath, Wulf, and Nierhoff-Wielk, Barbara, eds
Ex Machina: Early Computer Graphics up to 1970
Munich, 2007

Leavitt, Ruth, ed.
Artist and Computer
New York, 1976

Mason, Catherine
A Computer in the Art Room: the Origins of British Computer Arts 1950–1980
Norfolk, 2008

Reichardt, Jasia, ed.
Cybernetic Serendipity: the Computer and the Arts, Studio International
special issue
London, 1968

Reichardt, Jasia
The Computer in Art
London, 1971

Wands, Bruce
Art of the Digital Age
London, 2006

Digital Images

The patterns reproduced in this book are stored on the accompanying compact disc as jpeg files (at approximately A5-size, 300 dpi). You should be able to open them, and manipulate them, direct from the CD-ROM in most modern image software (on Windows or Mac platforms), and no installation should be required (although we, as publishers, cannot guarantee absolutely that the disc will be accessible for every computer).

Instructions for tracing and tiling the images will be found with the documentation for your software.

The names of the files correspond to the V&A inventory numbers of the images.